GREEN FUN

GREEN FUN

PLANTS AS PLAY

MARIANNE HAUG GJERSVIK

FIREFLY BOOKS

A FIREFLY BOOK

Published by Firefly Books 1997
Copyright © 1997 by Marianne Gjersvik

Cataloguing-in-Publication Data

Gjersvik, Marianne
      Green Fun
ISBN 1-55209-105-8 (bound)
ISBN 1-55209-096-5 (pbk.)
1. Nature craft – Juvenile literature.   I. Title

TT160.G56 1997   j745.58'4   C96 932478-2

"4745.5" OK per sm 1/98

Published by
Firefly Books Ltd.
3680 Victoria Park Avenue
Willowdale, Ontario
Canada   M2H 3K1

Published in the U.S. by
Firefly Books (U.S.) Inc.
P.O. Box 1338, Ellicott Station
Buffalo, New York 14205 U.S.A.

Design by Counterpunch/Linda Gustafson
Printed and bound in Canada by Friesens, Altona, Manitoba

Printed on acid-free paper

Poem on page 21 from HUNDREDS OF FIREFLIES by Brad Leithauser
Copyright © 1981   Reprinted by permission of Alfred A. Knopf Inc.

To my children and grandchildren. They are the reason all this matters. And to my mother and father who passed on their love of nature and the outdoors.

This collection has been assembled from memory, a few things from books, but mainly from the recollections of lots of people who told me about the fun they had with plants. They not only gave me information but also shared their pleasures and happiness.

Thanks to all of you.

The author has tried to be as accurate as possible with information. We regret any errors or omissions.

CONTENTS

Introduction	1
Acorn Whistle	2
Burdock Baskets	4
Buttercups	5
Clover Chains	6
Collecting	7
Crown of Flowers	8, 9
Daisies	10
Dandelion Curls	11
Dandelions	12, 13
Fairy Rings and Handkerchiefs	14
Geranium Fingernails	15
Grass Whistle	16
Grass Foxtail Caterpillar	17
Hollyhock Dolls	18, 19
Lamb's Ears	20
Looking	21
Maple Leaf Crown	22, 23
Maple Seed Polly Noses	24
Milkweed Boat	25
Milkweed Wishing Bug	26, 27
Money Plant	28
Pansy Faces	29
Paint from Plants	30
Plantain Violin	31
Poisonous Plants	32
Pussy Willows	34
Rose Bud Bird	35
Smells and Scents	36
Snapdragon Puppets	37
Sunflowers	38
Thistle Tassel	39
Violet Princess	40
Your Own Green Fun	41

GREEN FUN

INTRODUCTION

D id you ever make a squawky whistle out of a blade of grass? If you did, you'll know the sort of activity this book is all about. It is about making playthings with leaves and flowers and weeds, using just your hands and no equipment or other supplies.

In every garden, field, lawn, woodland, and even in city sidewalks, you can find absolutely free materials for an endless number of simple activities with which to amuse and delight yourself and whoever is with you, whether a child, a grandchild, or a person from any generation. You won't need a knife, or glue, or string, or scissors or anything except some quiet time, patient hands, and some leaves or flowers.

In the past, this information was passed from child to child and it's how I learned many of these amusements. Some of the information came from books but most of this material came from casual conversations with people who told me about the things they did when they were young. They shared information and, most important, happy memories. Because these activities are free and available to everyone and easy to do, there are no bad memories of deprivations or inadequacies. They are usually done outdoors in nice weather and so thoughts of very pleasant times are evoked.

One of the earliest lessons to teach children about plants is: "Not in your mouth." This is good advice for all ages. Don't put any plants in your mouth unless you are absolutely sure they are safe to eat.

And now, in the tradition of folklore, I take this opportunity to tell you about these pleasures and hope that you will pass the information along to others.

As you do these simple entertainments, be thankful for the bounty and beauty of the plant world.

To the gardener

If you allow people to use the plants in your garden for play, you might find some favorite blossoms picked and torn apart and left wilted at the end of the day. Many serious gardeners find this hard to deal with, but I ask you to consider that the most beautiful flowers will die in a few days anyway. Those flowers that were picked and played with will live forever in memory. They will live long after the flowers and the garden are gone and will be remembered with pleasure and affection for nature and for the person who created the garden.

ACORN WHISTLE

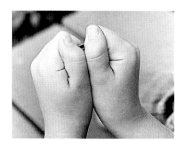

A loud piercing whistle can be made using an acorn cup. The first thing to do is to find an acorn cup that is about 3/4 inch in diameter. Red Oaks have the right size acorns. The best way to find the acorns is to look carefully while you are taking walks on autumn days. When you spot a few on the ground, you can be sure there are lots more nearby. Look around and collect all you can for future use. This in itself is a fine way to spend some time.

To make the whistle, start by putting your thumbs over the open cup. Now separate the top joints of your thumbs to leave a V-shaped opening over the cup. With your lips pursed, blow hard into the hole as if you were blowing into a flute.

Some people do this easily but others have to keep trying till they get the feel of directing a focused stream of air down into the hole in just the right way. With some patience and quite a bit of shifting of the position of your mouth, your thumbs, and the acorn cup, you will eventually get the right sound.

When you are able to do this, you will find that the sound produced is so loud it will bother most people's ears. This usually pleases children.

FINGER PUPPETS

Transform your fingers into little puppets by putting the acorn cups on the tops of your fingers and then marking little faces on them using the natural paint from pokeberry juice. Crush a few of the berries in an acorn cup, dip a thin stick in the juice, and use it to draw with.

      Don't ever put the pokeberry juice into your mouth. Even though Native Americans used this juice to decorate their faces, it is poisonous so be careful how you handle it.

Great oaks from little acorns grow.

BURDOCK BASKETS

Arctium minu

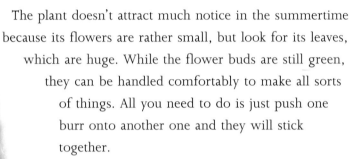

Anyone who has walked wild areas in the autumn knows about burrs. They are the dried seeds of the burdock flower and they have spiny projections with little hooks on the ends that catch onto clothing if you brush by them. The product "velcro" works on the same principle of having little hooks attach to material.

The plant doesn't attract much notice in the summertime because its flowers are rather small, but look for its leaves, which are huge. While the flower buds are still green, they can be handled comfortably to make all sorts of things. All you need to do is just push one burr onto another one and they will stick together.

The little basket pictured was made to hold some blackberries that grew nearby. Some of the burrs had a little bit of the purple flower showing which added to the attractiveness of the basket. You could also make doll furniture or a funny space ship or anything else you can imagine.

BUTTERCUPS

Ranunculus acris

They say that you can tell if a person likes butter by holding a buttercup blossom under a person's chin and then judging the intensity of the reflection of the yellow color. If the color is strong, then that is supposed to mean the person likes butter.

CLOVER CHAINS

Trifolium repens

Clover leaves normally have three segments. Once in a while there will be one with four segments. It's considered good luck to find such a four-leafed clover.

Long-stemmed white clover can be used to make a necklace or a long chain. Pick some clover with long stems. Now make a slit at the end of the stem with your fingernail. Thread the next stem through the hole and then make a slit in that stem and thread another clover through. Continue this process till you have a chain as long as you like to make your necklace. Make a larger hole in the end stem and then pull the first blossom through that hole like a button through a buttonhole.

I was told by an acquaintance that, as a child in New Orleans, she and her friends made clover chains that stretched the length of her street, just for fun.

COLLECTING

Sometimes it's fun just to collect lots of "something" from nature. It can be flowers or leaves or seeds. You can collect seeds of all sizes. There are very tiny seeds like those of Portulacas that are almost as fine as dust. The seeds are in a tiny little seed capsule. Take off the tiny lid and inside are the seeds.

In autumn, the huge seeds of the horse chestnut tree fall on the ground for you and the squirrels to collect. They are very smooth and nice to hold. If you rub them on the side of your nose, which is oily, they will become even more shiny.

Sometimes you can find Chinese lanterns, and then there are acorns in all sizes. Nature is very generous so collect the seeds you want and enjoy having them. When you're tired of them, scatter them as a way of planting them in some special place of your own.

You can also collect petals of sweet-smelling flowers or the leaves of strong-smelling herbs like mint and anise-hyssop and let them dry. This kind of fragrant dried collection is called a "potpourri."

CROWN OF FLOWERS

To make a crown or wreath of flowers, gather a bunch of flowers with stems at least six inches long. Begin by holding one flower stem horizontally with the flower to the left.

Place another flower vertically behind the first one. Bend the stem of this second flower up over in front of the stem of the first and around behind its own blossom so that the second stem lies alongside the first.

If you look at the illustration carefully, it will probably be easier to understand these directions. Continue to add flowers till you have the length you want. Then overlap the ends of the wreath and join them with some shorter stemmed flowers using the same method as before but tucking in the loose short ends to hold it all together.

Some flowers that can be used to make this type of crown are daisies, pink clover, Coreopsis, Cosmos, Queen Anne's lace, black-eyed Susans or Artemisia branches. Almost any flowers with stems that can be cut to five inches long can be used.

In Scandinavia, people make flower crowns to wear in celebration of Midsummer Eve, which is the summer solstice or about June 21.

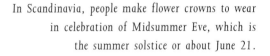

DAISIES

Chrysanthemum leucanthemum

Many people have played, "he loves me, he loves me not" with a single daisy blossom. You just pick off one petal at a time saying the words, "he loves me, he loves me not" and the words you are saying when you get to the last petal on the center of the flower predict how your intended feels about you.

The word daisy comes from the contraction of the words, day's eye.

Daisy crowns are made in the same way as the flower crowns on page 8 and 9.

You can make a lady with a bonnet by using your fingernail to cut all the petals of the daisy short except for two which form the ribbons of the bonnet. The face is made by using a fine stick to poke holes to represent eyes, nose, and mouth in the yellow center of the flower.

You can make a little rabbit face by taking all the petals off except two for the ears of your make-believe bunny.

DANDELION CURLS

Taraxacum officinale

If you split the stems of the dandelion into long strips by cutting through them with your fingernail and then dip them in water, they will twist into beautiful loops and curls which might turn out useful to children without curls of their own.

DANDELIONS

Taraxacum officinale

Some people call dandelions "weeds" but I like to think of them as wildflowers. When they bloom in early springtime, children are allowed to pick all they want. They make swell bouquets to give to moms and other friends.

When I was a child, we called dandelions "pee-in-the-bed" (the French call them *pissenlit*). Supposedly, if you picked them, they would have the effect of making you wet your bed. This worried me and took some of the pleasure out of picking them. This is absolutely not true but it seems there is a basis for this name. Dandelion leaves are actually a diuretic and in olden times were used as such.

The word dandelion comes from the contraction of the French words *dents de lion*, which means teeth of the lion. This is because the jagged edges of the leaves are said to look like lion's teeth.

The Dandelion

"Oh Dandelion yellow as gold
what do you do all day?"
"I wait and wait in the tall
green grass till the
children come to play."

"Oh Dandelion yellow as gold
what do you do all night?"
"I wait and wait in the
tall cool grass till my hair
grows long and white."

"And what do you do when
your hair is white and the
children come to play?"
"They pick me up in their
dimpled hands and
blow my hair away."

From an old Reader

If the blossoms aren't picked, a fluffy round seed head forms and if you blow on it, the seeds fly away and fall to earth like little parachutes. Some say that if you blow away as many seeds as you can in one breath and then count the number of seeds left on the stalk, it tells you either what time it is or the number of children you will have.

FAIRY RINGS AND HANDKERCHIEFS

If you see mushrooms in the lawn in the form of a circle, it's called a fairy ring. If you see a patch of cobweb floating on some leaves, it's called a fairy handkerchief. Fairy folk are often said to sit on or hide under mushrooms and toadstools.

Are there such beings as fairies, elves, gnomes, leprechauns or devas? Folklore says there are. Lots of people say there are. People say that even if you don't see them, you can see the results of their activities. They are said to be the ones who "hide" the things you lose. It's said they're like the wind. You can't see it but you can feel it's there.

Are all these beings only in people's imagination? Maybe. Then again, maybe not. It's all in how you look at it. It appears they are usually considered very pleasant company.

I like to fill my woods with elfs and fairies, sprites and gnomes and feel their presence as I sit or walk. To me they are friendly, busy little people sharing my enjoyment and multiplying the pleasures of my rambles abroad.

Ernest H. Wilson
If I were to make a garden,
1903

GERANIUM FINGERNAILS

Pelargonium

hen I was young, fingernail polish was definitely forbidden for children. But we would spend hours making our own version of nail polish using geranium petals.

Pull the individual petals from the flowers. Now, one by one, coat the underside of them with saliva and press them on your fingernails. They will stick there looking like nail polish. I could never decorate all ten fingers because by the time I got about eight petals on, the first would begin to dry and fall off. Maybe you can do better than I did.

GRASS WHISTLE

You can make a very loud, squawky whistle using a wide blade of grass, not lawn type grass but wide coarse grass that grows in weedy places. Hold the grass blade with both hands, stretching it between the tips and the bases of your thumbs. With your lips against the space just below your thumb knuckles, blow very hard into your hands across the blade of grass. Be sure the grass is stretched tightly across the inside of the opening. Young children's hands are usually too softly formed and there may not be a space below their thumb joints so they may not be able to do this.

I've heard that there are people who can actually blow a tune this way. I suppose they do that by changing the shape of the hollow formed by the rest of the hand behind the thumb opening.

GRASS FOXTAIL CATERPILLAR

Phleum alpinum

The seed heads of foxtail grass kind of look like caterpillars. Break the seed heads off close and lay them across the palm of your hand. Now, gently tense and relax your palm slightly in a cupping motion. As you do this, the "caterpillar" will move across your palm.

WEEDLE-RING

Pull the foxtail stem out from the base of the grass. Circle the stem once or twice around your finger leaving the ring a bit larger than your finger. Take if off your finger holding the shape. Then take the remaining stem and wrap it over and under the ring to hold it together. You could take off the seed head but I rather like it in place.

A little girl wrote to me saying she had invented this.

HOLLYHOCK DOLLS

Althaea rosea

To make a doll from hollyhocks, pick two closed buds and one open blossom. Poke a thin stick or twig partway into the base of the open flower. Then push one bud onto the projecting stick. Attach another bud on top of the first one to make a head. It sometimes is easier if you first make the holes into the buds before you assemble them. Use short twigs poked into the middle bud to represent the arms. These twigs are from an old mock orange bush. If you can't find thin twigs, you could use toothpicks to assemble your doll.

Look for other small flowers to use for a hat. The hat in the photograph is a mock orange blossom.

LAMB'S EARS

Stachys byzantina

he fuzzy gray leaves of this lovely plant are shaped like a little lamb's ears. Pick some of them and feel how very soft and velvety they are.

LOOKING

One of the very best things to do outdoors is just to look. If you sit quietly and patiently almost anywhere outdoors, you will find something that is special. It could be colors in the flowers and leaves. It might be the textures of the bark of the trees. Small children find that endlessly interesting. Paying attention is how you see more and learn more.

"Merely
to watch, and say nothing,
gratefully,
is what is best, is
what we needed."

Brad Leithauser, excerpt from
   "Hundreds of Fireflies"

MAPLE LEAF CROWN

B reak the stems off a bunch of leaves and put them aside to use as "pins." Now put one leaf partly overlapping another and then attach it by using a single stem to pin through the center ribs of the leaves. Add more leaves the same way, one at a time, till you have a band long enough to reach around the person's head. When the size is right, connect the first leaf to the last with another "pin" and your crown is ready to wear.

MAPLE SEED POLLY NOSES

D ifferent types of maple trees have different types of seeds. The Norway maple has big flat seeds that, while they are still green, can be used to make a "polly nose." Break them in half and peel apart the flat seed area and you will find that it is sticky inside. Spread the sides apart and press it onto the end of your nose. You will have what some people think looks like a parrot's beak. Parrots are sometimes called "polly" and so you have your "polly nose." This is also called a "Pinocchio nose" for obvious reasons.

Another kind of maple tree has smaller seeds with rounder seed areas. If you throw those in the air, they will spin to earth like little helicopters.

MILKWEED BOAT

Asclepias syriaca

Milkweed has seed pods that contain fluffy white fibers that are sometimes used as a filling for pillows the way down is used. When the seed is released, the fibers open to form a kind of parachute to carry the seed away.

If you peel away the outside of the milkweed pod before it is quite ripe, you will find what looks like a fish, scales and all.

The pod itself can become a sail boat, or even a little cradle.

MILKWEED WISHING BUG

Asclepias syriaca

Pull the fluff out of the milkweed pods and toss it high into the air. If the day is sunny, the sky deep blue, and there is a little breeze, then you will have a most wonderful sight.

Try to catch one of the little puffs, hold it cupped in your hands and make a wish. Then, let it float off into the air carrying your wish with it. And so children call it a wishing bug.

MONEY PLANT

Lunaria annua

In the springtime, the money plant starts out as a very nice, light purple flower. When the seeds form and then turn dry, they take the shape of discs with a thin brown layer on each side of the disc. When you rub away the brown dry layers, the seeds will also fall away and then left behind is a silvery translucent white disc. You could make believe that they are coins.

PANSY FACES

Pansies are flowers that seem to have faces. Johnny-jump-ups are a related plant that is smaller but they too seem to have faces. Pick a few different sizes and ones that have different markings and you will have a collection of flowers that are a collection of characters who may remind you of people you know.

PAINT FROM PLANTS

There are some plants from which you can get a kind of paint. If you take the faded flowers from Spiderwort or Tradescantia and crush them, the fluid from them will be a very nice blue color. You could paint a little water color sketch with it.

Another is Celandine. When you break one of the stems, the sap or fluid that comes from the stem is brilliant yellow. You can draw with it on a piece of paper. You can also draw in red with the stems of bloodroot.

These colorful juices from plants can be harmful so be careful not to get any on your skin and certainly not in your mouth!

PLANTAIN VIOLIN

Plantago major

Sometimes called a "bullfrog fiddle," this violin is made from a big leaf of the plantain weed. With your fingernails, slice partway through the top side of the stem. Gently pull it apart a little way and you will see the strings of the fiddle.

Native Americans called this variety of plantain "white man's footsteps." This plant wasn't native to America, but wherever English settlers went, they brought along the seeds.

POISONOUS PLANTS

One of the first things to teach very young children is that they shouldn't put any plants in their mouths. While still young, they won't be able to tell the difference between the plants that are safe to eat and handle and the ones that can be harmful. Once you learn which plants can be harmful, it starts to seem that lots of them are, one way or another. Unless you have someone knowledgeable tell you what is safe to eat, it's still best not to eat any plants. You can enjoy them and handle them but just be prudent.

Even the beautiful lily of the valley is poisonous to eat.

Pokeweed berries, leaves, and roots are poisonous so never put them in your mouth.

Mushrooms are beautiful to look at but again, it's better not to
touch them unless you really know what they are. Some of
the prettiest ones are not safe to handle, although they
are very tempting to touch and play with. Better to
be safe and just enjoy looking at them; don't
handle them or put them in your mouth.

One of the plants that is not good to even touch is poison ivy.
Most people will get an itchy, uncomfortable rash from having
it even brush against them. Make it a point to learn what it
looks like. Poison ivy is a vine that usually grows over
stone walls and up trees. It has a distinctive pattern
of three leaves. In the autumn, the leaves turn a
bright red. One of the few times I spray to
eliminate a plant from the garden is when
I see poison ivy.

PUSSY WILLOWS

Salix discolor

When the pussy willows show their soft gray catkins, it is one of the first signs that spring has really come. Just stroking them is a pleasant thing to do. You can break them off their stems and make believe they are tiny kittens or tiny mice. People sometimes paste them on a piece of paper and draw little tails on the end of them.

When the soft gray catkin matures, the pollen forms on it and it is now a little yellow "kitten."

ROSE BUD BIRD

* *

Rosaceae

P ick a rose bud that is still fairly closed. Pinch or cut the
stem close to the base of the flower, leaving about 1/4 inch.
Now break off two of the sepals at the base of the bud.
Turn the bud horizontally and poke two thin twigs into the petals
to represent the feet and there's your bird.

People who grow roses are not always willing to
have someone pick their treasures but if you explain
your purpose nicely, maybe they will let you have a
few. Sometimes you can find some wild roses
rambling over a fence where people won't
mind if you pick a bunch.

SMELLS AND SCENTS

Many flowers and leaves smell delicious. Almost all plants have some smell if you get very close, but then there are those that have a strong odor that they are known for. Various plants smell stronger either early or late in the day.

In the spring, lily of the valley and lilacs start the fragrant year. With summer there are sweet-smelling flowers of all kinds. The crushed leaves of peppermint and spearmint offer spicy smells. Lavender not only smells good when in bloom but it will hold its fragrance even when dried. Many people put pleasant-smelling dried plants in drawers or closets to have the good smell all year.

Then there are the plants that have a terrible odor. Skunk cabbage leaves smell just like a skunk!

The soft leafy tips of the sassafras smell like sweet candy. Sassafras is sometimes called the mitten tree because some of the leaves look like mittens.

SNAPDRAGON PUPPETS

Antirrhinum majus

S napdragon blossoms can be made to look as if they were "talking." Gently squeeze the sides of the flower. The upper and lower parts will open and close like a mouth. Depending on how you hold the flower, it can seem to have different expressions.

What in the world would flowers have to say if you could hear them?

This trick can also be done with the yellow flowers of a wild plant called butter and eggs, which looks like tiny snapdragon flowers.

SUNFLOWERS

Helianthus 'Mammoth Russian'

Sunflower seeds make for good eating. It's rather tedious to shell them but the kernel tastes good. Birds especially like sunflower seeds. If you put one of these huge seed-filled flower heads where you can watch it, you will see blue jays and cardinals having a feast.

THISTLE TASSEL

Cirsium vulgare

aking a thistle tassel is not a simple thing to do. It takes great care and patience and manual dexterity but if you succeed, you will have a very fine tassel.

It would probably be best to cut the flower with clippers or scissors. Then, very carefully, peel away the spines covering the area from which the flower emerges. As you can see from the photo, it can be done but it is best left to people with quite a bit of skill. If you manage to do it, you will have a beautiful item and you can be quite proud of yourself.

VIOLET PRINCESS

Violaceae

In early springtime, there are often violets growing in the wild places along roads and fields. Take one of the flowers and pull off the two lower side petals. Now turn the flower upside down and if you look closely, you will see what looks like a tiny princess on a throne wearing a big purple skirt.

Pick a bunch of violets in early spring and surround the flowers with a ring of the heart-shaped leaves. Then tie them together with a blade of strong grass. This miniature bouquet was called a "tussie-mussie" in olden times.

YOUR OWN GREEN FUN

o you know things that I haven't written about?
Use this page to record your own
memories and pleasures.

Design and art direction: Counterpunch / Linda Gustafson
Editorial: Maraya Raduha
Jacket separation and film: Batten Graphics
Text separation and film: Embassy Graphics
Printing and binding: Friesen Printers

This book is typeset in Joanna, designed in 1930 by Eric Gill,
and named after his daughter, Joan. The display type is Lithos,
designed in 1989 by Carol Twombly.